Communities
Living in a
Suburb

by Lisa Trumbauer

Consulting Editor: Gail Saunders-Smith, PhD

Capstone
press
Mankato, Minnesota

Pebble Books are published by Capstone Press,
151 Good Counsel Drive, P.O. Box 669, Mankato, Minnesota 56002.
www.capstonepress.com

1 2 3 4 5 6 10 09 08 07 06 05

Library of Congress Cataloging-in-Publication Data
Trumbauer, Lisa, 1963–
    Living in a suburb / by Lisa Trumbauer.
    p. cm.—(Communities)
    Includes bibliographical references and index.
    ISBN 0-7368-3632-2 (hardcover)
    1. Suburban life—Juvenile literature. I. Title. II. Communities (Mankato, Minn.)
HT351.T78 2005
307.74—dc22
                                                    2004011162

Summary: Simple text and photographs describe life in suburbs.

Note to Parents and Teachers

The Communities set supports social studies standards related to people, places, and geography. This book describes and illustrates suburbs. The images support early readers in understanding the text. The repetition of words and phrases helps early readers learn new words. This book also introduces early readers to subject-specific vocabulary words, which are defined in the Glossary section. Early readers may need assistance to read some words and to use the Table of Contents, Glossary, Read More, Internet Sites, and Index sections of the book.

Table of Contents

Suburbs

A suburb is a community outside or near a city. Many suburbs can be near the same city.

A suburb is
much like a city.
But suburbs have
less traffic than cities.

A suburb has
many neighborhoods.
The houses look the same
in some neighborhoods.

Some neighborhoods
have apartments
and townhouses.

28

12

Work and School

Some people live
in suburbs and drive
to cities to work.
Other people ride buses.

Some people work in
offices in suburbs.
Some children go
to schools in suburbs.

Fun in a Suburb

Suburbs have malls.
Malls have many shops
and places to eat.

Suburbs have parks.
People have fun
with family and friends.

Many suburbs are near
each big city.
Do you live in a suburb?

Glossary

apartment—a building divided into rooms where people live

community—a group of people who live in the same area

mall—a large indoor shopping center with many stores

neighborhood—a small area within a community where people live

townhouse—a house that is connected to other houses

traffic—moving vehicles; traffic includes cars, taxis, buses, trucks, and bicycles.

Read More

Holland, Gini. *I Live in the City.* Where I Live. Milwaukee: Weekly Reader Early Learning Library, 2004.

Miller, Jake. *Who's Who in a Suburban Community.* Communities at Work. New York: PowerKids Press, 2005.

Trumbauer, Lisa. *Communities.* Mankato, Minn.: Yellow Umbrella Books, 2001.

Internet Sites

FactHound offers a safe, fun way to find Internet sites related to this book. All of the sites on FactHound have been researched by our staff.

Here's how:

1. Visit *www.facthound.com*
2. Type in this special code **0736836322** for age-appropriate sites. Or enter a search word related to this book for a more general search.
3. Click on the **Fetch It** button.

FactHound will fetch the best sites for you!

23

Index

Word Count: 114
Grade: 1
Early-Intervention Level: 13

Editorial Credits

Mari C. Schuh, editor; Kate Opseth, designer; Jo Miller, photo researcher; Scott Thoms, photo editor

Photo Credits

Bruce Coleman Inc./Jan Stromme, 1; David Madison, 4
Capstone Press/Karon Dubke, cover, 12, 14
Corbis/Chris Daniels, 8; Robert Holmes, 16
The Image Finders/Mark E. Gibson, 20
OneBlueShoe, 6
Steven J. Meunier, 10, 18